Johannes
BRAHMS

PIANO CONCERTO No. 1
IN D MINOR
Op. 15

Edited by
Clinton F. Nieweg
Robert Sutherland

Study Score
Partitur

PETRUCCI LIBRARY PRESS

Duration: ca.45 minutes

First performance: January 22, 1859
Hannover, Kgl. Hoftheater
Johannes Brahms, piano
Hoftheater Hofkapelle / Joseph Joachim

ISMN: 979-0-58021-146-0

Concerto No. 1 for Piano in D minor, Opus 15

Johannes Brahms

Johannes Brahms' *Piano Concerto No. 1* has a fascinating compositional history. It was initially composed as a sonata for two pianos in 1854. Realizing its symphonic nature, the composer set about reworking the piece as a Symphony but found his efforts unsatisfactory. Not wanting to give up the original idea of a piano sound, in 1856 Brahms finally gave the work the form of a concerto for piano and orchestra. For this purpose Brahms used material from the symphony's first movement and wrote two new movements resulting in its present form; Maestoso, Adagio, and Rondo: Allegro non troppo. He finished work on the concerto in March, 1858 and was continually revising it until its premiere in Hanover, Germany on January 22, 1859, conducted by Joseph Joachim with the composer as soloist, to polite, if unenthusiastic, applause. Five days later it received its Leipzig premiere at the Gewandhaus to scorn and hisses, which must have been a shock to Brahms who did not think of himself as being ahead of his time as a composer. Yet this work is less of a concerto in the traditional sense; a virtuosic showpiece with orchestral accompaniment, as a symphony for piano and orchestra. While the solo part is indeed virtuosic, much of its role is as a musical equal to the orchestra in the stating and development of thematic material.

The editors' primary purpose is to provide an accurate performing edition of this work. To that purpose available sources were studied, a list of the major disparities among editions have been noted, and the orchestral material and full score have been edited such that no rehearsal time need be wasted in checking notation. The problematic treble and bass clef notation in the Horn II and IV parts has been changed to treble clef for the low "C" to avoid confusion.

Brahms himself created the piano four hands version of the concerto so it is considered a primary source when preparing the solo piano part for performance. This part as it appears in the full score corresponds to the piano four hands version published by Breitkopf und Härtel as edited by Otto Singer. The C.F. Peters edition for piano four hands was edited by Emil von Sauer.

Brahms made many alterations to the work before deciding to have it published. It was initially turned down by Breitkopf und Härtel as a result of the audience reception in Leipzig. Rieter-Biedermann published the piano part in 1861 and the orchestral material in 1862. Brahms sent Rieter-Biedermann a transcription for piano four hands on February 11, 1864 with a request that he not be credited as the arranger. The full score was not published until 1873. Brahms' manuscript of the full score is housed at the Deusche Staatsbibliothek in Berlin. The Brahms Institute features digitized copies of some of the original publications at the URL:

< http://www.brahms-institut.de/web/bihl_notenschrank/ausgaben/op_015.html>.

Robert Sutherland

Comments Regarding Disparities between Score and Parts Sources

This chart is a listing of major differences between the available sources. All obvious engraving errors have been corrected without comment. The editors, after careful study of the sources, have made the decisions printed in this corrected edition, while the comments below provide conductors with the necessary information to make further decisions on their own.

Sources:

1. Original piano edition with orchestra cues: *Concert für das Pianoforte mit Begleitung des Orchesters, Op.15.*
   Winterthur: J. Rieter-Biedermann, n.d.[1861]. Plate 170, 53 pages.
2. Original edition score and parts: *Concert für das Pianoforte mit Begleitung des Orchesters ... Op.15.* Partitur.
   Leipzig; Winterthur: J. Rieter-Biedermann, 1873. Plate 815, 175 pages.
3. Full score and Parts, ed. Eusebius Mandyczewski, Hans Gál.
   Leipzig: Breitkopf & Härtel, 1927, Plates Part.-B. 3210 (score), Orch.-B. 2810 (parts)
   reissued – Wiesbaden: Breitkopf & Härtel, 1991, Partitur PB 3210, Orchesterstimmen OB 3210, Studienpartitur 3654.
   reprinted – Huntington Station, L.I., N.Y.: E.F. Kalmus & Co., Inc.. n.d.(after 1933); Boca Raton: E.F. Kalmus, LC, 1989. A1345
5. Studienpartitur, ed. Paul Badura-Skoda. London: Eulenburg, n.d.[ca.1963], Plate E.E. 4564, Ed. Eulenburg No.713.
6. *Concert für das Pianoforte mit Begleitung des Orchesters, Op.15.* <Zu vier Händen.> [Arranged by the composer.]
   Leipzig; Winterthur: J. Rieter-Biedermann, n.d.[1864].
   reprinted – Mineola, NY: Dover Publications, 1996)
7. 2 piano 4-hand reduction, ed. Otto Singer.
   Leipzig: Breitkopf & Härtel, n.d. plate 29815, EB 6043
8. 2 piano 4-hand reduction, ed. Emil von Sauer
   Leipzig: C.F. Peters, n.d. plate 10153, EP 3655
9. Brahms' personal copies of the printed scores as held by the Gesellschaft für Musikfreunde, Vienna

The soloist will use either source 7 the Breitkopf or source 8 the Peters 2-piano 4-hand reduction. The solo piano part in the Breitkopf edition most closely corresponds to the Breitkopf/Kalmus full score reprint A1345. Conductors should be aware that there are minor differences in articulations, dynamics and notes between the three engravings and only the major ones are listed below.

In the orchestra parts the indication Solo = the beginning of a solo passage for the Piano.
The indication (Solo) = an important passage for that part's instrument.

Status Code	SCORE Page	Instrument	Mvt.	Meas. #	Beat	Comments refer to the original score and parts unless stated.
	7	Horns I & II in D	I	7-10; also 229-232; 311-319	4	Brahms used "old notation" with the notes in bass clef to be read an octave higher; i.e. the written C in measure 1 is the same pitch as the written C in measure 7. In many passages the correct octave is shown in the part in treble clef and in the score in bass clef. The corrected 2010 edition Horn I part is now written in treble clef.
?	3	Viola	I	35		Violin I has con sord. Viola does not. If added to the viola a senza sord. could be placed at measure 52. Conductor's decision.
	3	Viola	I	47		Lower Viola: The simile is for the articulation and slurring as in measure 46.
	4	Violin II	I	53	3, 4	The notation in the part has been corrected to match the notional abbreviation in the score sources.
?	6	Viola	I	76	2+	Add f to match the Violin and WW dynamics? If used add ff at measure 79 beat 2+. Conductor's decision.
?	11	Bass	I	138-141 etc.		In the R-B and Breitkopf engravings the musical lines that descend below the low E string for basses are written up the octave. The exception being the R-B separate Contrabass part where a low E flat is engraved by mistake in measure 48, beat 5. When the Bass C extension is available these measures can be played down an octave to continue the cello line. Conductor's decision..
	12	Viola	I	150-151	3,4	The notation in the part has been corrected to match the notional abbreviation in the score sources.
	14	Woodwinds, Horns	I	183		A diminuendo in this measure occurs in the piano reductions. Compare with measure 407.
	14	Horn III, IV in F	I	184-185		The slur in this measure (from G to C) is notated only for horns. Confirmed by the sources.
	15	Violin II	I	186	2,3	The slurred phrase C to G, then separate G has been corrected in the 2010 edition. See measure 410.

	17	Upper Strings	I	200		Slur to measure 201 like measure 424 to 425. Parts have been adjusted to match the original Violin 1.
?	20	Strings	I	244, 246		The Cello and Bass lines have a crescendo sign marked in all editions but the Violins and Violas do not. This crescendo sign appears in the piano reductions marked "Str." and in the R-B piano conductor score but not in the Brahms 4-hand piano reduction. Should all strings crescendo? Conductor's decision.
	23	Bassoon II	I	286	1	Score has B in octave with Bassoon 1. Part has C sharp in unison with the piano solo. Decision: B should read C sharp, based on study of the sources.
	26	Tutti	I	302	1	Editorial dynamics shown in ( ) were added by the Breitkopf engraver. Only the *p* in Viola and Cello are in the autograph. R-B has *p* in measure 301 continuing in measure 302 with no crescendo.
	27	Tutti	I	306, 307	1,3,5	Strings are marked staccato for bowing. Winds are not so marked. The staccatos engraved by mistake in Trumpets and Timpani in measure 306, beat 3 and 6 has been removed. No staccato in R-B.
	35	Clarinet I	I	399	6	The Clarinet solo entrance (Concert F natural) which is shown in the Breitkopf score has been added to the part in this 2010 edition. This anacrusis is not in the autograph or the Breitkopf part but is in the Solo Piano line. Also see Flute measure 175, beat 6.
	41	Winds	I	455	4	An [*f*] has been added as notated in the strings to show the cresc to measure 460.
	41	Tutti	I	459		The unusual *ff* on beat 1 has been removed to allow the cresc to measure 460. The Brahms 4-hand piano reduction has a continual cresc from measure 456 to 461.
	42	Piano solo	I	470	1	The chord is voiced differently in the piano reductions from the R-B piano conductor score and the Brahms 4-hand piano reduction.
	43	Violins 1, 2	I	478	1	The original parts have an accent on beat 1. This has been removed as per the notation in the score sources.
?	45	Viola	II	1		The *[con sord.]* at the beginning of the movement and the *[senza sord.]* before the Rondo is an editorial marking. The use of the mute will allow the Violas to correspond with the tone color of the Violins. Biedermann piano reduction score gives "Viol. col Sordini. Peters piano reduction has "Br., Vl. con sord." Conductor's decision.
	45	Oboe	II	8		The word Fl. in the margin has been corrected to the word Ob. as the passage from 9 to 11 is correctly engraved in the Oboe part.
?	46	Solo Piano	II	21	1	The half note (A) octave in the left hand is engraved in the Breitkopf and Eulenburg scores. This note is not in the Breitkopf and Peters piano reductions.
?	50	Bass	II	59	1	Should the dynamic *p* read *f* like the horns in order to match the cello dynamic in measure 61? All piano reductions have *f* for the bass line. Conductor's decision.
	51	Horn I, II in D	II	74	3-6	In measure 74, beat 3 to 5 sound the same although the notation makes it look like beat 5 is an octave lower.
	52	Tutti	II	82		This measure is split over two lines in the score; numbered as 82 for beats 1, 2, 3 and (82) for beats 4, 5, 6.
	52	Bassoon II	II	83	5	The word *dim.* added by the original engraver has been deleted. The *dim* sign is in measure 84.
	53	Flutes, Oboe	II	84, 85		The Flutes play in octaves and the Oboe rests from beat 5 on in the autograph. See Eulenburg score page 89. The music line as shown is that given in the Breitkopf score and parts.
?	55	Violins	III	9, 13, 36, etc.	2+	Use *Nachslag* or *Ohne Nachslag*? The notation of the grace notes after the trills varies from edition to edition. The Brahms 4-hand piano reduction uses the *Nachslag* to finish the trills. Conductor's decision.
?	59	Cello	III	87, 89		A crescendo sign is shown in the R-B part and the Brahms 4-hand piano reduction. This dynamic is not in the R-B score, Breitkopf score or Breitkopf/Peters piano reductions. At measure 90 the *p crescendo* in the R-B part matches the dynamics of the other string sections. Conductor's decision.
	65	Bassoon II	III	176	1 to 2	Score has G, **G**, F sharrp. Part has G, **A**, F sharp like the Basses. Decision: G should read A based on study of the sources.
	70	Woodwinds	III	283, 284		"Hairpin" dynamics are shown as given in the Brahms 4-hand piano reduction, and the Breitkopf and Peters piano reductions.
	70	Tutti	III	285, 286		Cresc. notated in autograph and piano reductions.
	72	Bass	III	305	1	Dynamic *p* added as in the piano reductions.
	72	Solo Piano	III	311-317		An "ossia" version by Emil von Sauer [?] is shown in the Peters piano reduction. Not in the Breitkopf piano reduction.

| ? | 73 | Solo Piano | III | 325 | 1 | LH: Notes engraved in the Breitkopf score: G, B-flat, **A, F**. Notes in the R-B engraving, Peters and Breitkopf piano reductions: G, B-flat , **F, A**. |
| | 75 | Viola | III | 339 | 1+ | The *f* should read *ff* as engraved in the R-B piano conductor and the Brahms 4-hand piano reduction. |

Prepared by: Robert Sutherland, Chief Librarian, Metropolitan Opera and Clinton F. Nieweg   *Date: 1988 to 2010*
This edition would not have been possible without the implementation of the corrections by Carol Westfall, the Editorial Assistant for the Nieweg Editions.
Acknowledgements: Robert O'Brien, Nancy M. Bradburd, David J. Miller

Status codes:
? – A questionable correction to be made at the conductor's discretion. s/r = should read. R-B = J. Rieter-Biedermann piano [conductor] first edition.
The editors welcome any additions, corrections, or comments to this edition. Contact: Proofferr@comcast.net

ORCHESTRA

2 Flutes

2 Oboe

2 Clarinets (B-flat and A)

2 Bassoons

4 Horns (D, B-flat basso, F)

2 Trumpets (D)

Timpani (D and A)

Violins I

Violins II

Violas

Cellos

Double Basses

(Transposed Clarinets, Horns, and Trumpets parts are published)

Concerto No. 1
for Piano and Orchestra
Op. 15

Johannes Brahms
Edited by Clinton F. Nieweg and Robert Sutherland

11
Fl.
Ob.
Klar. (B)
Fag.
(D) Hr. (B)
Trpt. (D)
Pk.
1.Viol.
2.Viol.
Br.
Vcl.
K.-B.
21
a 2
espr.

31
Fl.
Ob.
Klar. (B)
Fag.
(D)
Hr.
(B)
1.Viol.
2.Viol.
Br.
Vcl.
K.-B.
pp
dim.
con sord.
pp legato
espr.
41
A
div.
sim.
p
pp

48
Fl.
Ob.
Klar. (B)
Fag.
Hr. 3. (B) 4.
1.Viol.
2.Viol.
Br.
Vcl.
K.-B.
54
Fl.
Ob.
Klar. (B)
Fag.
(D) Hr. (B)
1.Viol.
2.Viol.
Br.
Vcl.
K.-B.
dim.
p marc.

62
A1
Fl.
Ob.
Klar. (B)
Fag.
(D) Hr. (B)
Trpt. (D)
Pk.
1.Viol.
2.Viol.
Br.
Vcl.
K.-B.
1.
senza sord.
senza sord.
ff marc.
ff sempre
cresc.
69
A1

76
Fl.
Ob.
Klar. (B)
Fag.
a2
[ff]
(D) Hr. (B)
Trpt. (D)
Pk.
1.Viol.
2.Viol.
Br.
Vcl.
K.-B.
82
dim.

87
B
Fl.
Fag.
Hr. 1. (D) 2.
1.2.
Trpt. (D)
p dim.
Pk.
Klav.
p espr.
1.Viol.
2.Viol.
Br.
Vcl.
K.-B.
pizz.
p
pp
93
pizz.
pp

98
Hr. 1.
(D) 2.
1.2.
pp
Trpt.
(D)
pp
pp
Pk.
pp
Klav.
1.Viol.
arco
pp
2.Viol.
arco
pp
Br.
arco
pp
Vcl.
pp
K.-B.
102
Klav.
cresc.
cresc.
1.Viol.
2.Viol.
Br.
cresc.
Vcl.
ben marc.
cresc.
K. B.

106
Klav.
molto cresc.
1.Viol.
2.Viol.
Br.
Vcl.
K.-B.
110
Fl.
a 2
Ob.
Klar. (B)
Fag.
Hr. 1. (D) 2.
1.2.
Pk.
arco

C
118
Fl.
Ob.
Klar. (B)
Fag.
a 2
(D) Hr. (B)
mutano in F
Trpt. (D)
Pk.
Klav.
espr.
1.Viol.
2.Viol.
Br.
Vcl.
K.-B.
pizz.
C
124
Hr. 1. (D) 2.
1.2.
Trpt. (D)
Pk.
Klav.
1.Viol.
2.Viol.
Br.
Vcl.
K.-B.

129
Klar. (B)
Hr. 1. (D) 2.
Trpt. (D)
Pk.
Klav.
1.Viol.
2.Viol.
Br.
Vcl.
K.-B.
1.2.
1.
pp
più p
134
Fl.
Klar. (B)
Hr. (D) 1.
Klav.
1.Viol.
2.Viol.
Br.
Vcl.
K.-B.
dim.
arco
pp

142
C1
Fl.
Ob.
Klar. (B)
Hr. 3. (F) 4.
3.4. in F
Klav.
1.Viol.
2.Viol.
Br.
Vcl.
K.-B.
147
a 2
Solo
Fag.
arco
cresc.

153
Ob.
Fag.
Hr. 3.
(F) 4.
Klav.
1.Viol.
2.Viol.
Br.
Vcl.
K.-B.
f
dim.
p dim.
157
Poco più moderato
espr.
p legato
164
p dolce
168
cresc.
171
f
dim.
Ped.

174
1. Solo
Fl.
Ob.
Klar. (B)
Fag.
Solo
pp
a 2
p
1. Solo
Klav.
1.Viol.
2.Viol.
Br.
Vcl.
K.-B.
178
C2
Hr. 3. (F) 4.
3.4.
p espr.

185
Klav.
p legato
9
cresc.
1.Viol.
2.Viol.
Br.
Vcl.
K.-B.
189
Fl.
Ob.
Klar. (B)
Fag.
Hr. 1. (D) 2.
1. 2.
a 2
f marc.
f
mf

193
Fl.
Ob.
Klar (B)
Fag.
(D) Hr. (F)
Klav.
1.Viol.
2.Viol.
Br.
Vcl.
K.-B.
f
f marc.
mf marc.
mf
196
Klar. (B)
Fag.
Hr. 3. 4. (F)
p
pp
p marc. ma dolce
dim.
1.
4.

200
Klar. (B)
Fag.
Hr. 3. (F) 4.
Klav.
p
più f
1.Viol.
2.Viol.
Br.
Vcl.
K.-B.
pizz.
pizz.
arco
pp
pp
pp
204
cresc.
f
dim.
legato
dim.

207
Hr. 3. (F) 4.
Solo
marc. ma dolce
p
4.
pp
Klav.
dim.
dolce
p
1.Viol.
(ein Pult)
pp
dim.
2.Viol.
Br.
Vcl.
K.-B.
211
Hr. 3. (F) 4.
3.
4.
p
a 2
Klav.
216
Fl.
1.
pp
Ob.
pp
1.
pp
Klar. (B)
pp
Fag.
pp
pp
mutano in B basso
Hr. 3. (F) 4.
3.
4.
pp
1.Viol.
Tutti
pp
2.Viol.
pp
Br.
pp
Vcl.
pp
arco
K.-B.
pp

C3 Tempo I
226
Fl.
Ob.
Klar. (B)
Fag.
Hr. 1. (D) 2.
Trpt. (D)
Pk.
Klav.
1.Viol.
2.Viol.
Br.
Vcl.
K.-B.
p cresc.
ff
mf
molto cresc.
C3 Tempo I
231
Hr.
cresc.

237
Ob.
Klar. (B)
Fag.
Klav.
1.Viol.
2 Viol.
Br.
Vcl.
K.-B.
ff
p
mf
cresc.
cresc. molto
242
Fl.
Ob.
Klar. (B)
Fag.
Hr. 1. (D) 2.
1.2.
pp cresc.
f
Klav.
ff
1.Viol.
2.Viol.
Br.
Vcl.
K.-B.

247
Fl.
Ob.
Klar. (B)
Fag.
Hr. 1. (D) 2.
Trpt. (D)
Pk.
Klav.
1.Viol.
2.Viol.
Br.
Vcl.
K.-B.
C4
252
fp dim.
pp
p espr.
C4

261
Fl.
Klar. (B)
Fag.
Hr. 1. (D) 2.
Klav.
1. Viol.
2. Viol.
Br.
Vcl.
K.-B.
pp
p espr.
270
Ob.
dim.

278
D
Ob.
Fag.
Hr. 1.
(D) 2.
Klav.
1.Viol.
2.Viol.
Br.
Vcl.
K.-B.
a 2
mf
f
ff
pizz.
arco
D
283
Fl.
Ob.
Klar.
(B)
Fag.
Hr. 1.
(D) 2.
Trpt.
(D)
Pk.
Klav.
1.Viol.
2.Viol.
Br.
Vcl.
K.-B.
pp cresc.
p cresc.
p
pp
f
mf
p legg.
pizz.

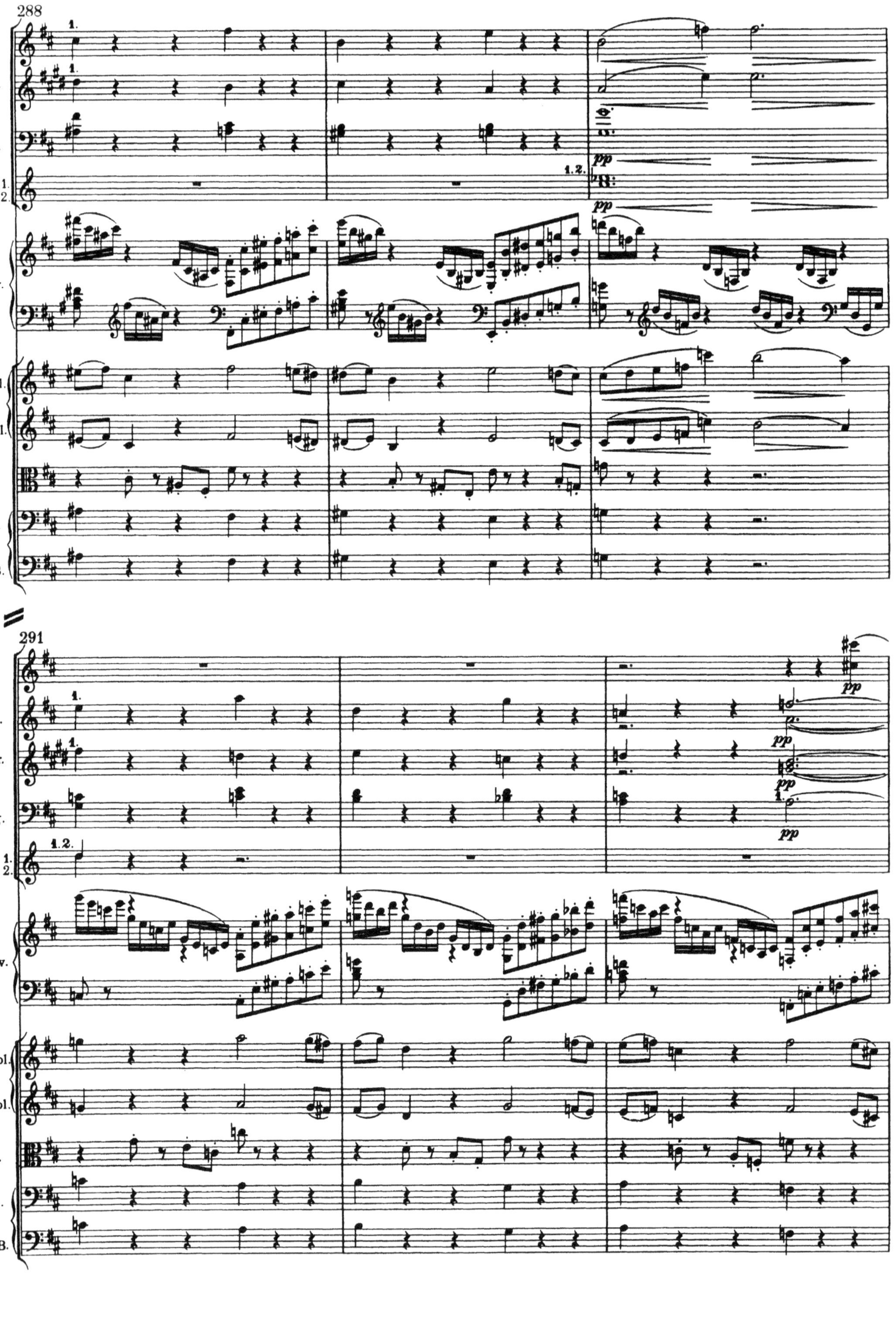
288
Ob.
Klar. (B)
Fag.
Hr. 1. (D) 2.
Klav.
1.Viol.
2.Viol.
Br.
Vcl.
K.-B.
pp
1.2.
291
Fl.

294
Fl.
Ob.
Klar. (B)
Fag.
Hr. 1. (D) 2.
Klav.
1.Viol.
2.Viol.
Br.
Vcl.
K.-B.
pizz.
297
Solo
Trpt. (D)
Pk.
p marc.
a 2
div. arco
pp legg.
marc.
arco
(p) arco
K.-B

302
Fl.
(pp)
Ob.
a 2
(p)
Klar. (B)
(p)
Fag.
(pp)
(D)
Hr.
(B)
cresc.
Trpt. (D)
p
Pk.
cresc.
Klav.
p
cresc.
8
1.Viol.
(pp)
pp
cresc.
2.Viol.
(pp)
pp
cresc.
Br.
p
mf cresc.
Vcl.
p
pp
cresc.
K.-B.
cresc.

306
E
Fl.
Ob.
Klar.
(B)
Fag.
(D)
Hr.
(B)
Trpt.
(D)
Pk.
Klav.
1.Viol.
2.Viol.
Br.
Vcl.
K.-B.
ff
f
mf
p
tr
E

313
Fl.
Ob.
Klar.
(B)
Fag.
Hr. 1.
(D) 2.
Pk.
Klav.
1.Viol.
2.Viol.
Br.
Vcl.
K.-B.
321
pp cresc.
[pp] cresc.

329
Fl.
Ob.
Klar. (B)
Fag.
Hr. 1. 2. (D)
Trpt. (D)
Pk.
Klav.
1.Viol.
2.Viol.
Br.
Vcl.
K.-B.
a 2
ff con forza
336
a 2

E1
339
Fl.
Ob.
Klar.
(B)
a 2
Fag.
(D)
Hr.
(B)
p cresc.
Trpt.
(D)
Pk.
ff
mf
fz
Klav.
1.Viol.
2.Viol.
Br.
Vcl.
K.-B.
pizz.
E1

343
Fl.
dim.
p
Ob.
dim.
Klar. (B)
dim.
p
Fag.
dim.
(D)
Hr.
(B)
p marc.
Trpt. (D)
p
Pk.
p
pp
tr
Klav.
p
1. Viol.
dim.
p
2. Viol.
dim.
p
Br.
dim.
p
Vcl.
dim.
p
K.-B.
dim.
p

347
Fl.
Ob.
Fag.
Hr. 1. (D) 2.
Klav.
1.Viol.
2.Viol.
Br.
Vcl.
K.-B.
a 2
pp
p
espr.
1.2.
pizz.
arco
351
Klar. (B)
1.
p marc.

354
F
Fl.
Klar. (B)
Fag.
Hr. 1. (D) 2.
Klav.
1.Viol.
2.Viol.
Br.
Vcl.
K.-B.
pizz.
pp sempre
358
pp
poco f
arco
p

362
Klav.
dim.
p dolce
p
Vcl.
pp
K.-B.
pp
367
Klav.
Vcl.
K.-B.
372
Fl.
a 2
p
Ob.
Solo 1.
p poco cresc.
Klar. (B)
Solo 1.
p
poco cresc.
Fag.
p
poco cresc.
Hr. 1. (D) 2.
Solo 1.
p poco cresc.
Klav.
tr
cresc.
1.Viol.
p
poco cresc.
2.Viol.
p
poco cresc.
Br.
p
poco cresc.
Vcl.
p
poco cresc.
K.-B.
p
poco cresc.

377
Ob.
Fag.
Hr. 1. (D) 2.
Klav.
f
dim.
1.Viol.
2.Viol.
Br.
Vcl.
K.-B.
381
Poco più moderato
p espr.
cresc.
388
p dolce
392
cresc.
f
396
Klar. (B)
Solo
p
dim.
dim.

400
G
a 2
Fl.
pp
Ob.
1.
pp
Klar. (B)
p
Solo
1.
Fag.
p
(D)
Hr.
(B)
3.
pp
Klav.
407
Fl.
Ob.
Klar. (B)
Fag.
Hr. 1. (D) 2.
Klav.
p legato
1.Viol.
p espr.
2.Viol.
p espr.
Br.
p espr.
Vcl.
p
K.-B.
p

412
Fl.
Ob.
Klar. (B)
Fag.
Klav.
cresc.
1.Viol.
2.Viol.
Br.
Vcl.
K.-B.
cresc.
416
Hr. 1. (D) 2.
1.2.
fp
mf marc.
f marc.
mf

419
Fl.
Ob.
Klar. (B)
Fag.
Hr. 1. (D) 2.
2.
p
pp
Klav.
dim.
1.Viol.
p
2.Viol.
p
Br.
Vcl.
dim.
pp
K.-B.
dim.
pp
423
Klar. (B)
pp
Fag.
1.
pp marc. ma dolce
Hr. 1. (D) 2.
1.2. Solo
pp
Klav.
p
espr.
cresc.
più f
1.Viol.
2.Viol.
pp
Br.
pp
Vcl.
pp
pizz.
K.-B.
pp
pizz.

427
Hr. 1.
(D) 2.
1.
pp
Klav.
cresc.
f
1.Viol.
pp
2.Viol.
Br.
pp
arco
Vcl.
pp
K.-B.
pp
430
3
legato dim.
dolce
18
18
(ein Pult)
pp
dim.
434
Solo
p marc. ma dolce
p
dim.
pizz.
p

438
Hr. 1. (D) 2.
1.2.
Pk.
p marc.
dim.
dim.
Klav.
pp dim.
dim.
Vcl.
arco
pp
K.-B.
arco
pp
444 Tempo I poco più animato
Klav.
p
più agitato
più f
cresc.
449
Fl.
f
ff
Ob.
f cresc.
ff
Klar. (B)
ff
Fag.
mf cresc.
ff
Hr. 1. (D) 2.
1.2.
p cresc.
ff
Trpt. (D)
f
Pk.
f
f
Klav.
fz
ff
(Alle)
1. Viol.
pizz.
arco
ff
2. Viol.
f
ff
Br.
ff
pizz.
arco
Vcl.
f
ff
arco
pizz.
K.-B.
f
ff

453
Fl.
Ob.
Klar. (B)
Fag.
(D) Hr. (B)
Trpt. (D)
Klav.
1.Viol.
2.Viol.
Br.
Vcl. K.-B.
unis.
cresc.
459
Fl.
Ob.
Klar. (B)
Fag.
(D) Hr. (B)
Trpt. (D)
Pk.
Klav.
1.Viol.
2.Viol.
Br.
Vcl.
K.-B.

464
Fl.
Ob.
Klar.
(B)
Fag.
(D)
Hr.
(B)
Klav.
1.Viol.
2.Viol.
Br.
Vcl.
K.-B.
469
Fl.
Ob.
Klar.
(B)
Fag.
a 2
(D)
Hr.
(B)
Klav.
1.Viol.
2.Viol.
Br.
Vcl.
K.-B.

473
a 2
Fag.
f
1.2.
Hr. 1.
(D) 2.
f
mf
Trpt.
(D)
mf
p
Pk.
mf
p
8
3
Klav.
ff
1.Viol.
f
mf
2.Viol.
f
mf
pizz.
Br.
f
pizz.
Vcl.
f
pizz.
K.-B.
f
476
1.2.
Hr. 1.
(D) 2.
cresc.
Trpt.
(D)
p
cresc.
Pk.
p
cresc.
8
Klav.
1.Viol.
mf cresc.
2.Viol.
mf cresc.
Br.
mf cresc.
Vcl.
mf cresc.
K.-B.
mf cresc.

479
Fl.
Ob.
Klar. (B)
Fag.
Hr. (D) (B)
Trpt. (D)
Pk.
Klav.
1.Viol.
2.Viol.
Br.
Vcl.
K.-B.
arco
arco
arco

Adagio
2 Flöten
2 Oboen
2 Klarinetten in A
2 Fagotte
Solo
pp legato
2 Hörner in D 1. 2.
1. p Solo
Pauken in D, A
Klavier
1. Violine
con sord.
p espr. e legato
2. Violine
con sord.
p espr. e legato
Bratsche
[con sord.] p espr. e legato
Violoncell
p
Kontrabaß
p
Adagio
8
Ob.
1. Solo
p
Klar. (A)
p
Fag.
Hr. (D)
2. p
Klav.
p molto dolce espr.
1.Viol.
2.Viol.
Br.
Vcl.
K.-B.

15
Fl.
Klar. (A)
Fag.
Hr. (D)
Klav.
1.Viol.
2.Viol.
Br.
Vcl.
K.-B.
1.
Solo
p
cresc.
dim.
pp
20
rf
cresc.
mf cresc.
mf

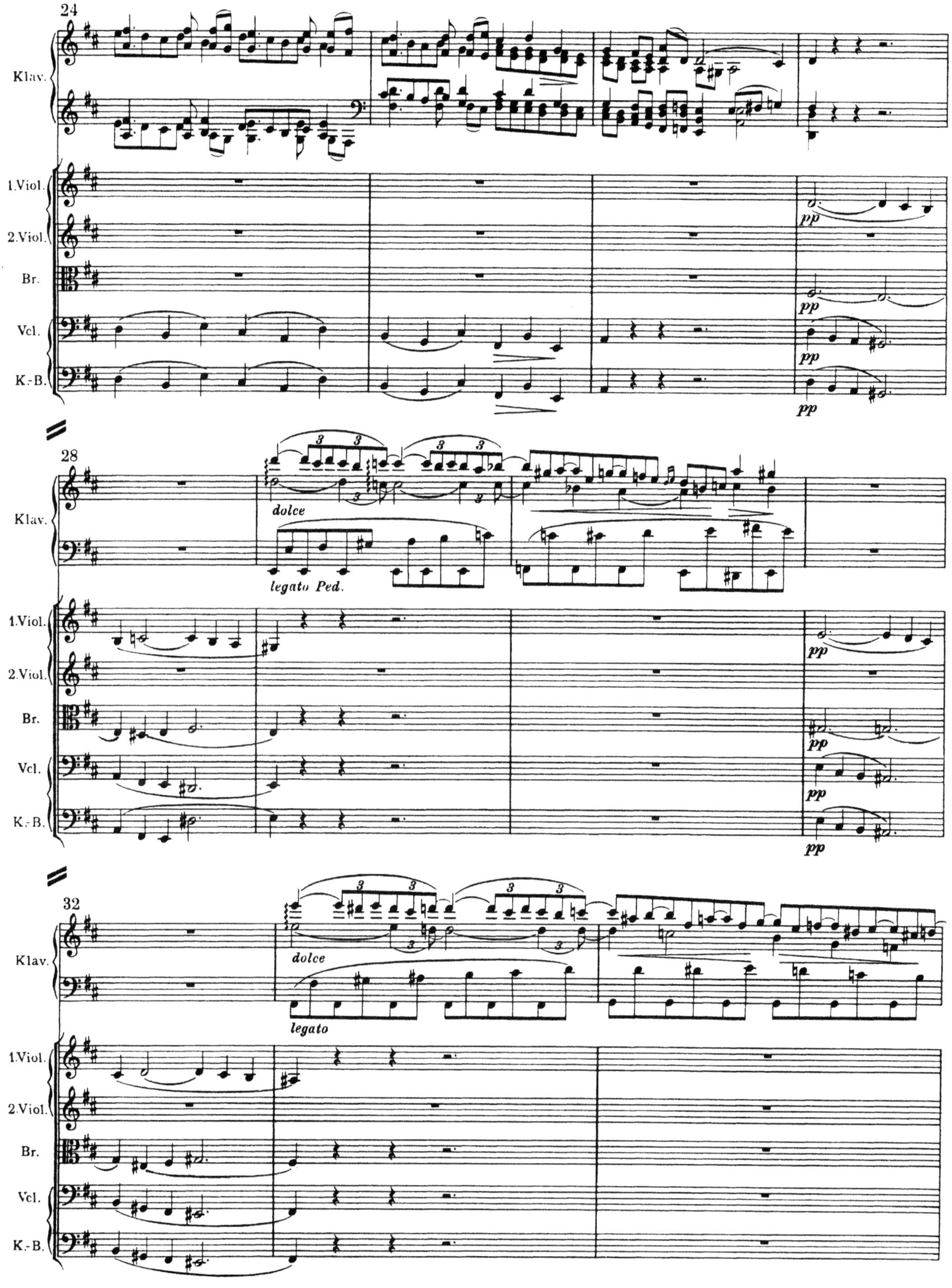
24
Klav.
1.Viol.
2.Viol.
Br.
Vcl.
K.-B.
pp
28
dolce
legato Ped.
32
legato

35
poco f
Klav.
38
Klav.
legato
41
Klav.
cresc.
6
dim.
44
A
a 2
Fl.
f
Ob.
f
Soli
Klar.
(A)
p
f
Fag.
p
f
Klav.
p
1.Viol.
f
2.Viol.
f
Br.
f
Vcl.
f
K.-B.
f
A

47
a 2
Fl.
Ob.
Klar. (A)
Fag.
Klav.
1.Viol.
2.Viol.
Br.
Vcl.
K.-B.
div.
50
Soli
53
p dolce

55
Klar. (A)
Fag.
Klav.
1.Viol.
2.Viol.
Br.
Vcl.
K.-B.
a 2
dim.
pp
p
B
58
1.
Ob.
Hr. (D)
p cresc.
f
p Solo
p espr.

66
Fl.
Ob.
Solo
1.
p
Klar. (A)
Fag.
Hr. (D)
2.
Klav.
molto espr. dolce
1.Viol.
2.Viol.
Br.
Vcl.
K.-B.
73
mf
f
molto cresc.
sf
molto cresc. sempre
legato
76
ff

C
79
a 2 Solo
a 2 Solo
1. Solo
Fl.
Ob.
Klar.
(A)
Fag.
Hr.
(D)
Klav.
Vcl.
K.-B.
ff
f
tr
C
81
82
a 2
1.
Klav.
(82)
a 2
a 2
1.

84
a 2
Fl.
dim.
p
Ob.
dim.
Klar.
(A)
Fag.
Hr.
(D)
1.
dim.
Klav.
dim.
1.Viol.
2.Viol.
Br.
pp
Vcl.
div.
pp
K.-B.
pp
87
Klav.
pp espr
legato
pp molto espr. e legato
1.Viol.
pp
2.Viol.
Br.
pp
Vcl.
pp
K.-B.
pp

92
Klav.
95
pp Cadenza ad lib.
molto Adagio
dim.
96
Fl.
Ob.
Klar. (A)
Solo
Fag.
Hr. (D)
Pk.
1.Viol.
pp espr.
2.Viol.
Br.
div.
Vcl.
K.-B.

Rondo
Allegro non troppo

2 Flöten	
2 Oboen	
2 Klarinetten in B	
2 Fagotte	
4 Hörner in D 1. 2. in B basso 3. 4.	
2 Trompeten in D	
Pauken in D, A	
Klavier	
1.Violine	
2.Violine	
Bratsche	
Violoncell	
Kontrabaß	

Allegro non troppo

8

Fl.	a 2
Ob.	
Fag.	
Hr. 1. (D) 2.	mf
Klav.	
1.Viol.	senza sord.
2.Viol.	senza sord. pizz. arco pizz.
Br.	[senza sord.] pizz.
Vcl.	pizz.
K.-B	pizz.

15
Fl.
Ob.
Fag.
1. Solo
p
Klav.
f
più dolce
1.Viol.
2.Viol.
Br.
Vcl.
K.-B.
22
1.
Fag.
Klav.
cresc.
29
1. 2.
Hr. 1.
(D) 2.
pp
Klav.
f
1.Viol.
2.Viol.
(pizz.)
Br.
f
(pizz.)
Vcl.
f
(pizz.)
K.-B.
f

35
A
Fl.
Ob.
Klar.
(B)
Fag.
(D)
Hr.
(B)
Trpt.
(D)
Pk.
Klav.
1.Viol.
2.Viol.
Br.
Vcl.
K.-B.
a 2
tr
arco
p dolce
42
Hr. 3.
(B) 4.
1.
3.
pp
p

50
Fl.
Ob.
1.
Klar. (B)
Fag.
Hr. 3. (B) 4.
3.
Klav.
1.Viol.
2.Viol.
Br.
Vcl.
pp
58
8. 4.
legato, dim. e dolce

A1
66
Hr. 3. (B) 4.
3.4.
espress.
Klav.
mf sempre cresc.
cresc.
Br.
Vcl.
pizz.
p
A1
72
Klav.
mf
Vcl.
arco
79
Klav.
f
Vcl.
pizz.
86
Fag.
p cresc. molto
Hr. 3. (B) 4.
3.4.
p cresc.
Klav.
poco f
f cresc.
1.Viol.
p cresc.
2.Viol.
p cresc.
Br.
p cresc.
Vcl.
arco
mf
p cresc.
K.-B.
p cresc.

93
B
Klar. (B)
Fag.
(D)
Hr.
(B)
Klav.
1. Viol.
2. Viol.
Br.
Vcl.
K.-B.
p dolce
p dolce
p dolce
B
102
Fl.
Ob.
Klar. (B)
Fag.
Hr. 3. (B) 4.
1. Viol.
2. Viol.
Br.
Vcl.
K.-B.
dim.
p dim.

114
Hr. 1. (D) 2.
Trpt. (D)
Pk.
Klav.
1.Viol.
2.Viol.
Br.
Vcl.
K.-B.
a 2
mf marc.
marc.
f
mf
pp cresc.
ff
pp
dim.
cresc.
trem.
124
Fl.
Ob.
Klar. (B)
Fag.
1.2.

128
Fl.
Ob.
Klar. (B)
Fag.
Hr. 1. (D) 2.
Trpt. (D)
Pk.
Klav.
1.Viol.
2.Viol.
Br.
Vcl.
K.-B.
pp
fp
p
1.2.
div.
133
138
143
molto cresc.
pizz.
f
tr

149
Klar. (B)
Fag.
Hr. 1. (D) 2.
Klav.
1.Viol.
2.Viol.
Br.
Vcl.
K.-B.
1.2.
a 2
1.
pp
tr
f
arco
p
pizz.
155
Fl.
sempre pp
cresc.

162
Hr. 1.
(D) 2.
2. p cresc.
Klav.
ff
167
C
Fl.
a 2
cresc.
ff
Ob.
Klar.
(B)
f cresc.
Fag.
(D)
Hr.
(B)
mf
1.Viol.
arco
2.Viol.
Br.
Vcl.
K.-B.
cresc.
C

174
a 2
tr
Fl.
Ob.
Klar. (B)
Fag.
(D)
Hr.
(B)
Trpt. (D)
Pk.
Klav.
1.Viol.
2.Viol.
Br.
Vcl.
K.-B.
ff
mf
fp
pp
p
espress.

184
Klar. (B)
Fag.
(D) Hr. (B)
Klav.
1.Viol.
2.Viol.
Br.
Vcl.
K.-B.
espress.
legato
pizz.
3.
D
197
Fl.
Klar. (B)
Fag.
Klav.
1.Viol.
2.Viol.
Br.
Vcl.
K.-B.
espress.
p dolce
pizz.
Solo
arco
D

208
Fl.
Ob.
Klar.
(B)
Fag.
Hr. 1.
(D) 2.
Klav.
1.Viol.
2.Viol.
Br.
Vcl.
K.-B.
pp
1. Solo
arco
dolce
pizz.
216
Solo pp
dim.
2.pp

224
Solo
Hr. 3. (B) 4.
3.4.
p
pp
Klav.
p dolce
1./2. Viol.
Br.
div.
pp
Vcl.
arco
p
K.-B.
arco
pp
231
3.4.
Hr. 3 (B) 4.
pp
Klav.
perdendosi
1./2. Viol.
Br.
div.
Vcl.
K.-B.
238
E
Klav.
1. Viol.
2. Viol.
p sempre
Br.
p sempre
Vcl.
p sempre
K.-B.
E

247
1.Viol.
2.Viol.
Br.
Vcl.
K.-B.
p sempre
marc.
255
Hr. 3.
(B) 4.
8. 4.
pp
cresc.
f
262
Fl.
Ob.
Klar.
(B)
Fag.
(D)
Hr.
(B)
1.Solo
a 2
perdendosi
pp sempre
dim.

269
Fl.
Ob.
Klar. (B)
Fag.
Hr. 1. (D) 2.
1.Viol.
2.Viol.
Br.
Vcl.
K.-B.
1.Solo
1.2.
pp
pizz.
arco
275
Klav.
283
cresc.
p cresc.
f

288
Klav.
292
Klav.
297
E¹
Fl.
Ob.
Klar. (B)
Fag.
Hr. 1. (D) 2.
Trpt. (D)
Pk.
Klav.
1.Viol.
2.Viol.
Br.
Vcl.
K.-B.
pizz.
E¹

302
Fl.
Ob.
Klar. (B)
Fag.
Hr. 1. (D) 2.
Trpt. (D)
Pk.
Klav.
1.Viol.
2.Viol.
Br.
Vcl.
K.-B.
arco
[p]
307
poco sostenuto
a tempo
Fl.
Klar. (B)
Fag.
Hr. 1. (D) 2.
Klav.
1.Viol.
2.Viol.
Br.
Vcl.
K.-B.
pizz.
pizz.
poco sostenuto
a tempo

312
Hr. 1. (D) 2.
Klav.
316
2. p
ff
320
F
Fl.
Ob.
Fag.
Trpt. (D)
Pk.
a2
f
mf
pizz.
arco
1.Viol.
2.Viol.
Br.
Vcl.
K.-B.
F

328
Fl.
Ob.
Klar.
(B)
Fag.
(D)
Hr.
(B)
Trpt.
(D)
Pk.
Klav.
1.Viol.
2.Viol.
Br.
Vcl.
K.-B.
a 2
ff
mf
f

335
Fl.
Ob.
Klar. (B)
Fag.
Hr. (D) (B)
Trpt. (D)
Pk.
Klav.
1.Viol.
2.Viol.
Br.
Vcl.
K.-B.
a 2
fp
f
tr
ff
sf
div.
unis.
f [f]

340
Fl.
Ob.
Klar. (B)
Fag.
Hr. 1. (D) 2.
Klav.
1.Viol.
2.Viol.
Br.
Vcl.
K.-B.
345
G
Trpt. (D)
Pk.
con passione
cresc.
pizz.
G

352
Klav.
1.Viol.
2.Viol.
Br.
Vcl.
K.-B.
arco
pp
pizz.
mf
358
f cresc.
cresc.
365
Fag.
Hr. 3. (B) 4.
Pk.
a 2
3.4.
f
p
tr
mf cresc.
ff
12

372
a 2
Fl.
Ob.
Klar.
(B)
muta in A
Fag.
(D)
Hr.
(B)
Trpt.
(D)
Pk.
Cadenza quasi Fantasia
Klav.
1.Viol.
2.Viol.
Br.
Vcl.
K.-B.
380
legato
sempre f
385
dim.

rit.
Klav.
f
p legato
cresc.
dim.
H a tempo
Fl.
Ob.
Klar.
(A)
Fag.
Hr. 1.
(D) 2.
Pk.
in A
a 2
espr.
Solo
p cresc.
pp
1.Viol.
2.Viol.
Br.
Vcl.
K.-B.
trem.

420
Fl.
Ob.
Klar. (A)
pp
Fag.
pp
a 2
(D)
Hr.
(B)
pp
Trpt. (D)
pp
tr
Pk.
pp
Klav.
p dolce
Ped.
1.Viol.
2.Viol.
trem.
Br.
pp
Vcl.
K.-B.

425
Fl.
Ob.
Klar. (A)
Fag.
(D)
Hr.
(B)
Trpt. (D)
Pk.
Klav.
1.Viol.
2.Viol.
Br.
Vcl.
K.-B.
a 2
Solo
cresc.
pizz.
cresc. poco a poco
pp
p

435
Fl.
Ob.
pp
Kla.
(A)
Fag.
a 2
(D)
Hr.
(B)
Trpt.
(D)
tr
Pk.
Klav.
p
1.Viol.
2.Viol.
arco
Br.
Vcl.
K.-B.

Meno mosso
440
Fl.
dim.
Ob.
dim.
p
molto dolce
Klar. (A)
dim.
a 2
Solo
a 2
Fag.
dim.
p dolce
dim.
(D)
Hr.
(B)
pp
[dim.]
p
Trpt. (D)
Pk.
dim.
p
Klav.
dim.
pp
1.Viol.
dim.
2.Viol.
dim.
Br.
dim.
Vcl.
dim.
p
K.-B.
dim.
Meno mosso

446
Fl.
Ob.
Fag.
Hr. 1. (D) 2.
Pk.
Klav.
1.Viol.
2.Viol.
Br.
Vcl.
K.-B.
molto dolce
p dolce
453
dim.
cresc.
1./2.Viol.
*)
Ausführung

460
Fl.
p cresc.
Ob.
p cresc.
Klar. (A)
p cresc.
Fag.
cresc.
Hr. 1. (D) 2.
1.
2.
cresc.
8
f
Klav.
463 Più animato
Fl.
Ob.
Klar. (A)
Fag.
Hr. 1. (D) 2.
1.2.
Klav.
f
cresc.
1.Viol.
arco
f
tr
cresc.
2.Viol.
arco
f
tr
cresc.
Br.
Vcl.
pizz.
f
K.-B.
Più animato

470
Ob.
Fag.
Klav.
1.Viol.
2.Viol.
Br.
Vcl.
K.-B.
mf
ff con forza
f
476
p cresc. poco a poco
sempre più f
cresc.
pizz.
p

482
Fl.
Ob.
Klar. (A)
Fag.
(D)
Hr.
(B)
Trpt. (D)
Pk.
Klav.
1.Viol.
2.Viol.
Br.
Vcl.
K.-B.
p cresc.
cresc.
arco
ff

489
Fl.
Ob.
Klar. (A)
Fag.
(D)
Hr.
(B)
Trpt. (D)
Pk.
Klav.
1.Viol.
2.Viol.
Br.
Vcl.
K.-B.
ff
f

495
Fl.
Ob.
Klar.
(A)
Fag.
(D)
Hr.
(B)
Trpt.
(D)
Pk.
f
Klav.
Cadenza ad lib.
accel.
1.Viol.
2.Viol.
Br.
Vcl.
K.-B.
502
f
510
molto accel.
ff

518
Tempo I
Fl.
Ob.
Klar. (A)
Fag.
Hr. (D)
(B)
Trpt. (D)
Pk.
Klav.
1.Viol.
2.Viol.
Br.
Vcl.
K.-B.
Solo
a 2
p cresc.
mf cresc.
cresc.
pizz.
arco
Tempo I

529
Fl.
Ob.
Klar. A)
Fag.
(D)
Hr.
(B)
Trpt. (D)
Pk.
Klav.
1.Viol.
2.Viol.
Br.
Vcl.
K.-B.
a 2
f
ff

www.ingramcontent.com/pod-product-compliance
Lightning Source LLC
LaVergne TN
LVHW081319060426

835509LV00015B/1593